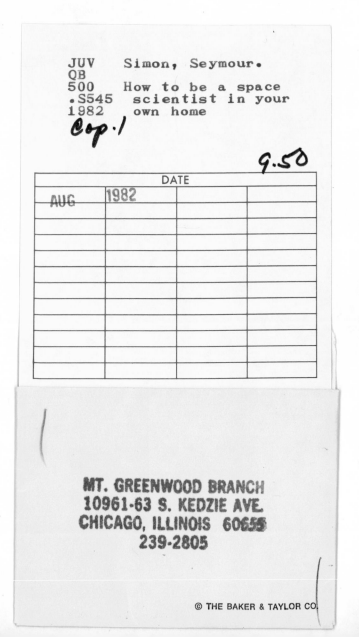

JUV   Simon, Seymour.
QB
500   How to be a space
.S545   scientist in your
1982   own home

Cop. 1

9.50

DATE			
AUG	1982		

How to Be a Space Scientist in Your Own Home

"How to Be a Space Scientist in Your Own Home"

by Seymour Simon

illustrated by Bill Morrison

J. B. Lippincott   New York

Many of the experiments in this book pre-
viously appeared in SCIENCE AT WORK:
PROJECTS IN SPACE SCIENCE, published by
Franklin Watts in 1971.

Library of Congress Cataloging in Publication Data

Simon, Seymour.
How to be a space scientist in your own home.
Biblio. Index.

Summary: A collection of experiments using
easily available, inexpensive materials, which
duplicate some principles and problems encountered
in space flight.
1. Space sciences—Experiments—Juvenile
literature. [1. Space sciences—Experiments.
2. Experiments] I. Morrison, Bill, 1935-   ., ill.
II. Title.
QB500.S545   1982   500.5'078   81-47759
ISBN 0-397-31990-8   AACR2
ISBN 0-397-31991-6 (lib. bdg.)

1 2 3 4 5 6 7 8 9 10

First Edition

Contents

Introduction   1

Your First Launch   3

Rocketing Ahead   6

Measuring Rocket Power   9

A Water-Powered Rocket   12

Fuel for Thought   15

How to Escape from Earth   18

Rocketing Steady   21

Going Down in Flames   24

Heat Shields   27

A Matter of Gravity   30

How to Lose Weight in Space   32

How to Gain Weight in Space   35

How Fast Is Your Spaceship?   38

Saturn Calling   41

Danger: Meteoroids Ahead   44

Empty Space   46

The Problem of Water   49

The Problem of Carbon Dioxide   52

Plants in Space   55

Magnetic Fields in Space   58

Is Anything Listening?   61

Star Light, Star Bright   64

Star Tracks   66

Are You Ready for Space?   69

Books For Reading and Research   73

Index   75

Glossary   79

How to Be a Space Scientist in Your Own Home

Introduction

You are living in the Space Age. Nowadays we rarely see a rocket launch on TV unless it's something special such as the first space shuttle. Many other satellite and space-probe launches hardly rate a paragraph in a daily newspaper. Is it possible that space science is getting to be too commonplace for anything puzzling or surprising to happen?

Not likely. Not when the Viking spaceships reveal that Mars has a surface unexpectedly like that of our moon. Or when the space probe Voyager discovers a ring around the planet Jupiter. Or when the space probe Pioneer shows us close-up pictures of the mysterious moons of Saturn. And who knows what we will discover when Halley's comet returns and a space-ship is there to meet it?

The world of outer space is still a challenging frontier. This book will help you to use and understand the principles and facts that space scientists use in their work. All you need are simple, easily available materials that you can find in and around your home. Then you can build models to find out how a rocket works, how to keep a spaceship on target, how a closed life-support system can exist in a spacecraft, how a radio beacon operates in space.

This book will show you how to be a space scientist in your own home!

Your First Launch

Here's What You Will Need: A wooden board about 6 inches wide and 10 inches long, rubber bands, three $\frac{1}{4}$-inch wooden dowels about 8 inches long or three pencils, three small nails, and tape.

Here's What to Do: Tape two of the dowels or pencils lengthwise on the board. Leave enough room between them for the third dowel. Drive two of the nails about halfway into the board about 5 inches apart, one on each side of the two dowels. Drive the other nail halfway into the third dowel. Place a rubber band between the two nails on the board. Place the third dowel between the other two.

Place the launcher on a table 4 feet high. CAUTION: *Be sure there is no one in the area into which the launcher points.* Pull the nail on the projectile back against the rubber band and release it. Measure the distance the dowel travels.

When an object falls freely from a height of four feet, it hits the ground in about half a second. The time it takes to reach the ground is the same no matter how fast the object is traveling in a horizontal direction. You can show this by dropping a dowel from the table at the same time that you launch another dowel. Both will hit the ground at the same instant.

For example, launch a dowel from a four-foot-high table. Suppose it travels ten feet ahead before it hits the floor (don't count bounces). Since the dowel falls four feet down in half a second, it has also shot ten feet forward in the same half a second.

You can use these numbers to find out how fast your dowel is flying in miles per hour. Here's how. If your dowel traveled ten feet in half a second, then it would have traveled twenty

4

feet in one second (twice as far). Multiply the twenty by 3600 (the number of seconds in one hour). That gives you 72,000 feet per hour. Divide that by 5,280 (the number of feet in a mile). That means that your dowel traveling at ten feet in half a second, is moving a bit more than thirteen and a half miles an hour.

Change the amount you stretch the rubber band. What happens when you pull it back farther? Does the dowel change its speed? Try using two or three rubber bands. Try changing the size and weight of the dowel. What happens now?

You may be surprised to find out that you are experimenting with the Second Law of Motion. It was first stated by Isaac Newton about three hundred years ago. The Second Law says (1) that the greater the force on an object the greater its change in speed or direction, and (2) that the heavier an object is the less its change in speed or direction.

This is easier to understand than it sounds. For example, it explains why you need more force to throw a baseball fast than you do to throw it slow. It also explains why it is easier to throw a light rock farther than a heavy rock. Now can you use the Second Law to help explain your launch results?

Rocketing Ahead

Here's What You Will Need: Paper matches, aluminum foil, a balloon, a straight pin, and a paper clip.

Here's What to Do: **Caution:** *Do this experiment in the kitchen sink or bathtub because it involves lighted matches.* Cut out a piece of aluminum foil 1 inch wide and $\frac{1}{2}$ inch longer than the match you're using. Place the match on the aluminum foil so that its bottom is even with the bottom end of the foil. Place the pin against the match so that its point is at the head of the match. Wrap the match and the pin in the foil, folding down a double thickness around the head of the match. Carefully pull out the pin, leaving an open channel under the foil from the head of the match to the bottom.

Bend the paper clip into a handle to hold the match at an angle, with its head uppermost. Place it in the tub or on a sink. Carefully hold a lighted match under the head of the foil-wrapped match until it lights.

When the chemicals in the match head start to burn, they change from a solid to a gas. The gas expands, pushing against all sides of the foil. The expanding gases can only escape in one direction, out the back. The match is forced in an opposite direction from the escaping gas.

This principle is called Newton's Third Law of Motion. It says that for every action, there is an equal and opposite reaction. Think about what you saw the match do. What was the action? What was the reaction?

Here's something else to try. Blow up a balloon with air, then let it go. In which direction does the balloon move? How can the Third Law of Motion help to explain what happens? How do you think you can make the balloon move faster and

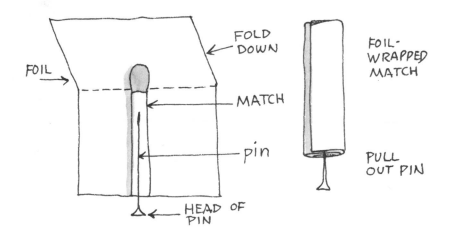

FOLD DOWN

FOIL

MATCH

pin

HEAD OF PIN

FOIL-WRAPPED MATCH

PULL OUT PIN

go farther? Try it without popping the balloon!

Your match rocket used a solid chemical rocket fuel. Modern rockets use either solid or liquid fuels. Solid fuels are safer to store and handle, but liquid fuels offer more power from the same amount of weight.

Liquid fuels can also be regulated in flight more easily than solid fuels. In most high-power space probes, liquid hydrogen is the fuel. Liquid oxygen, which helps fuel to burn, is also used. They are made by cooling oxygen and hydrogen gases to very low temperatures until they become liquids.

Measuring Rocket Power

Here's What You Will Need: A sensitive kitchen scale, a small empty plastic soda bottle with a cork to fit, a small pan, vinegar, water, bicarbonate of soda, measuring spoons, a paper napkin, a thumbtack and string.

Here's What to Do: Place the pan on the scale. Mix one tablespoon of vinegar with a cup of water and pour it into the soda bottle. Place the soda bottle on the pan and record the weight. Wrap a tablespoon of bicarbonate of soda in a square of a paper napkin. Insert the paper into the bottle and cork the bottle firmly immediately. CAUTION: *Do not push the cork in too tightly for the bottle may shatter.*

When the vinegar soaks through the paper and comes in contact with the bicarbonate of soda, a chemical reaction takes place. A gas, carbon dioxide, is produced. The expanding gas pushes the cork out of the bottle with a pop.

Watch the scale as the cork pops out. It will show the amount of thrust provided by the cork. Remember Newton's Third Law? How does that explain why the bottle is pushed downward?

This experiment measures thrust in much the same way that the thrust of large rockets is measured in static-test stands. What do you think are the advantages of a static test over launching a rocket each time you want to test its thrust?

Try experimenting with different amounts and proportions of the chemicals to increase the thrust of the rocket. Push a thumbtack into the top of the cork to increase its weight. Does this affect the amount of thrust? In what way?

If you do not mind cleaning up a little mess on the bathroom floor, try this. Tie a string around the neck of the bottle and another string around the body of the bottle. Pour in the vinegar. Tie the two strings on the shower head over the bathtub so that the bottle hangs sideways and swings freely. Insert the paper with the bicarbonate of soda and cork the bottle.

What do you expect to happen when the cork pops out? Try it and see.

A Water-Powered Rocket

Here's What You Will Need: A water rocket and hand pump (sold in many toy or hobby stores for a dollar or two), water, a scale, and a sweep-second-hand wristwatch.

Here's What to Do: You can prepare a water rocket for launch by first filling it about halfway with water and then using the hand pump to load the rocket with compressed air. Do not use more pressure than is written in the directions accompanying the rocket. Too much pressure may cause the plastic rocket to crack.

Launch your rocket in an open field so that you can easily retrieve it and so that it will not break on impact. CAUTION: *Never point the pumped-up rocket at anybody or at any part of your own body.*

One method of finding out how high your rocket goes is to time the interval in seconds between launch and landing. Then use the formula: $H = 16(\frac{t}{2})^2$ where H is the altitude, and t is the time in seconds. For example, let's say it took 4 seconds from launch to landing. You would first divide 4 by 2, which would give you 2. You would then square 2, giving 4 (you square a number by multiplying it by itself), and multiply this by 16. In this example, your rocket would have reached an approximate height of 64 feet.

Try using different amounts of water, but be sure not to exceed the limit on pressure. Would twice as much water launch a rocket to a higher or lower altitude? What influence does the air pressure have? Use fewer strokes of the hand pump and compare. Try to find out which combination of water and pressure gives you the longest flights.

Water rockets are also made in two-stage models. If you can

purchase one of these, you have even more of a chance to experiment. Does the same amount of water split between two stages instead of in one stage result in longer flights? What special problems do two-stage rockets present? What are the advantages and disadvantages of each kind of rocket?

Fuel for Thought

Here's What You Will Need: Copper sulfate crystals (found in many chemistry sets and can also be purchased in a drugstore), a Pyrex dish for use in an oven, a small jar with a cover, and half a small jarful of alcohol. CAUTION: *Alcohol is inflammable and should not be allowed near an open flame. Keep the alcohol covered.*

Here's What to Do: Place a small amount of the copper sulfate crystals in the Pyrex dish. Place the dish in an oven and set the temperature at about 500 ° F. Check every five or ten minutes until the chemical turns a pale gray color.

Use a pot holder to remove the dish from the oven, and turn the oven off. Place the copper sulfate crystals in a small jar and keep them tightly covered.

Now you can test for the presence of water in the alcohol, using a few crystals of copper sulfate at a time. Place one or two of the copper sulfate crystals in the alcohol sample. Cover the jar and shake.

If the alcohol contains water, the grayish-colored copper sulfate will turn blue. If no water is present, the copper sulfate will remain gray. Almost all alcohol has some water mixed in with it.

Rocket fuels must be made of very pure materials. Even small amounts of impurities, such as water, may cause problems in fuel burning. A reduced amount of rocket thrust may result from these impurities. This change can easily throw a rocket off course.

Of course rocket fuels may contain impurities other than water. Can you think of how you could get rid of solid impurities such as dust particles? How do you get rid of airborne dust particles if you have an air conditioner or hot air furnace?

Those kinds of cleaners are called filters. They act like strainers. Have you ever seen a filter used to clean the water in an aquarium? Can you explain how a filter works?

How to Escape from Earth

Here's What You Will Need: Poster cardboard or heavy construction paper, tape, a pile of books 1 foot high, and marbles.

Here's What to Do: Fasten one end of the poster cardboard to an edge of a table with tape. Bend the cardboard in a smooth curve and fasten the other end to the top of the book pile. The lower part of the cardboard should be nearly vertical while the upper part should be nearly horizontal.

Try releasing marbles from different points on the cardboard and observe how they fall. Try flicking a marble up the cardboard from different points.

The slope of the cardboard represents the gravitational pull of the earth. Because the lowest part of the cardboard is vertical, the marble falls rapidly at that point. This area represents the strong pull of gravity close to the surface of the earth.

A marble released at the top of the cardboard, where the curve is less, will roll slowly downward and pick up speed gradually. The top of the cardboard represents a place thousands of miles above the surface where the earth's gravitational pull is very slight.

Flicking the marble up the slope from the lower edge simulates the launch of a spacecraft. Try flicking the marble at different speeds. What effect does that have on the marble's path? Where is the most energy needed to pull away from the gravitational pull of the earth—near the surface or far away?

Starting a marble up the slope from a spot near the top of the cardboard represents the situation of launching a craft from an orbiting space station. What are the advantages of a launch point such as that?

How could you set up another pile of books and a cardboard

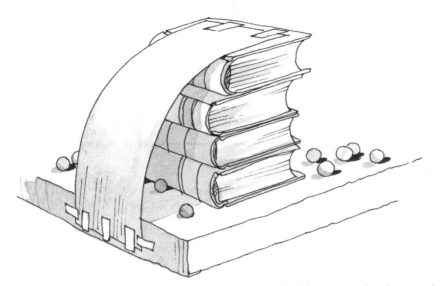

to represent the moon's gravitational field? How high would you make that pile of books if the moon's gravitational pull is only one-sixth as great as Earth's? How high would you make a pile of books to represent the planet Jupiter, whose gravitational pull is 2.64 times Earth's? Or the sun, whose gravitational pull is 26 times as great as Earth's?

Rocketing Steady

Here's What You Will Need: A toy top, a toy gyroscope, and string.

Here's What to Do: Stand the top on end and let go. Now set it spinning and set it on end. Observe the difference. Start a top gyroscope spinning. Try balancing it on the edge of a table. Hold one end of the spinning gyroscope and try to turn it in another direction.

Spacecraft can tip in three different ways when traveling forward. You can feel this kind of tipping if you try balancing a broom upright in the palm of your hand. In a spacecraft the rotating motion is called roll. A side-to-side motion is called yaw. An up-and-down motion is called pitch. Besides being upsetting to any astronauts aboard a spacecraft, these motions make flight guidance difficult and affect the way certain instruments work.

The spinning top or gyroscope shows one way to keep a spacecraft in a steady flight path. A spinning object tends to remain pointed in the direction of its axis (the line which it spins around). Because of this, spinning on an axis helps stop a spacecraft from wandering off course. For the same reason, a rifle barrel is grooved to spin a bullet as it shoots out. Can you think of the reason the earth does not wobble very much in its orbit around the sun?

What happens when you try to move a spinning gyroscope? Because a spacecraft needs to be stabilized in each of three directions, how many gyroscopes would you need aboard? How would you set them up in relation to each other?

If you have a bicycle wheel to use you can feel yourself being stabilized. Set a piece of broomstick on each end of the wheel axle to use as a handle. Hold on to one handle and spin the bicycle wheel as fast as you can. Now try to move the wheel in different directions. What happens?

Try sitting on a piano stool or a swivel chair with your feet off the ground. Twist the spinning bicycle wheel. What happens? Look at the heavy wheel of a toy gyroscope. Can you think of how you could make a bicycle-wheel gyroscope more effective?

Going Down in Flames

Here's What You Will Need: A block of wood, sandpaper, an air pump.

Here's What to Do: Rub the sandpaper over the block of wood. Touch the block of wood with your fingers. How does it feel? Rub the sandpaper more quickly over the wood. Do you notice any difference in how it feels?

Pump the air pump rapidly for a minute or two. Touch the bottom of the pump where the air is compressed. How does it feel?

When two surfaces rub together, they become heated because of the friction between them. The faster and harder the surfaces rub, the more heat is generated. This effect takes place even when you move through the air. Can you think of why you normally don't feel the heat of air friction?

Meteoroids are chunks of iron or rock that travel through space between the planets. When one of these chunks enters the earth's atmosphere, it begins to heat through friction. It begins to glow red hot and melt. The glowing gases that can be seen form a meteor. Some people call meteoroids shooting stars when they see them move across the night sky. Most meteoroids burn up and turn into gas before they get within fifty miles of the earth's surface.

A spaceship also travels very quickly. What do you think would happen if it were to plunge through the earth's atmosphere at top speed? Even airplanes, which travel at much slower speeds than spacecraft, experience temperature increase at their surfaces. Moving at 700 miles per hour, about the speed of sound, the temperature increases by about 95 ° F. The space shuttle travels at about 17,000 miles per hour when in orbit.

If the shuttle returned to the earth's atmosphere at that speed, surface temperatures might go up to about 3,000 ° F.

Make a list of different materials used at high temperatures around your home, such as in cooking utensils. Try to find out their melting temperatures from an encyclopedia or some other source. Which materials are likely to be used in the nose of the space shuttle? How do the passengers in such a craft live through the heat? Look at the next chapter to see one way the problem can be solved.

Heat Shields

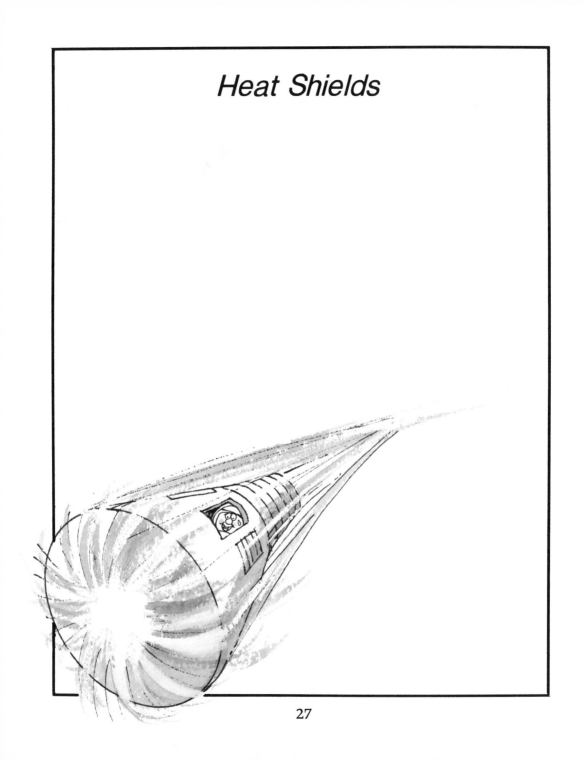

Here's What You Will Need: Two Pyrex test tubes or two baby (nursing) bottles, water, two thermometers, candle wax, an electric hot plate, a pan, and a double boiler.

Here's What to Do: Melt some candle wax in the top of a double boiler. Dip one of the test tubes or bottles in the melted wax and remove it. Allow the wax to harden. Do this several times, until a thick wax coating is built up.

Now fill each of the test tubes with an equal amount of cold water. Place a thermometer in each. Stand the test tubes in a pan of water on a hot plate. CAUTION: *Use the hot plate with care. Be sure to turn it off when you are finished with it.*

Heat the water in the pan. Note the temperature in each test tube every 30 seconds. Why does the water in the wax-coated test tube remain cooler than the water in the uncoated test tube? What happens to the wax as the water heats up? Could this kind of a heat shield be used more than once?

In the same way that the water remained cooler while the wax melted away, a spacecraft will remain cooler if it has a shield that melts away because of the atmosphere's friction. The material that melts away is called an ablation material, and the shield an ablation shield. The word "ablation" means removal.

In the capsules used in Mercury, Gemini, and Apollo missions, the ablation material coats the flat blunt end. Apollo spacecraft used a heat shield made of a special plastic held together by steel strips. The shuttle uses several heat shield materials, including a ceramic glass tile that is reusable.

Some of the heat-resistant materials discovered as a result of space research have been used in other ways. For example,

Pyroceram is a material used to make cookware that not only can stand high temperatures, but can also be put into water while red hot and still not crack. This material is sold under the commercial name of Corning Ware. Even specially treated glass such as Pyrex could not withstand such sudden heating and cooling. The nose cone materials of spacecraft are subjected to even more severe conditions.

A Matter of Gravity

Here's What You Will Need: A heavy rubber band, a small lead sinker or other weight, a wide-mouthed jar, and a pencil. *Here's What to Do:* Cut across the rubber band. Tie one end to the lead weight. Place the lead weight in the jar and lay the pencil across the top of the jar. Tie the other end of the rubber band around the pencil so that the weight is suspended about midway in the jar. Grasp the jar with both hands and move it sharply upward. Wait until the weight is again midway in the jar, and this time move the jar sharply downward.

When the weight is hanging midway in the jar, the pull of gravity downward equals the tension on the rubber band. What happens to the length of the rubber band when the jar is moved upward? What happens when the jar is moved downward?

The lead sinker can represent the weight of an astronaut. The jar moving suddenly upward represents the instant of a launch. The apparent weight of an astronaut increases during the launch. We say that g-forces are acting upon him. A force of two g's would increase his weight two times.

In an actual spacecraft launch, the g-forces are small at first. But they rapidly build up to about seven g's within two minutes. If an astronaut weighs 150 pounds on earth his weight at this time would be over 1,000 pounds.

At the end of a space flight, these forces may reach an even higher level than at launch, perhaps as much as twenty g's. Experiments have shown that a human body can stand as much as forty-five g's—but for only a split second.

How is the cabin of a spacecraft designed to protect an astronaut from the effects of g? Consult the works listed in "Books for Reading and Research" at the end of this book, to find out some of the ways.

How to Lose Weight in Space

Here's What You Will Need: A wide-mouthed jar, a heavy lead sinker, a rubber band, a pencil, a spring scale, and a friend to help you.

Here's What to Do: Cut a rubber band so that you have a single strand, and tie one end to the lead weight. Put the lead weight in a jar so that it rests on the bottom. Tie the other end of the rubber band around a pencil that has been placed across the top of the jar. The length of the rubber band should be adjusted so that it supports most of the weight of the sinker, so it just barely touches the bottom of the jar.

Hold the jar open end up, as high as possible, above a soft surface such as a mattress. Drop the jar and have a friend try to catch it before it hits.

Weightlessness does not mean that there is no gravity. In space, weightlessness occurs when a gravitational force is counterbalanced by the ship's motion. This happens during the time when the engines have stopped and the ship is coasting around the earth.

The lead sinker becomes weightless in relation to the jar during the time both are falling. Since the sinker is weightless, the stretched rubber band will pull it out of the jar while it is falling.

Still don't think that the sinker is weightless while it falls? Try this. Obtain a spring scale and hook the sinker onto it. Holding on to the scale, drop your hand rapidly. What happens to the weight shown on the scale during the time your hand drops? If your hand could drop fast enough, the weight would go to zero.

You can feel the same sensation of losing weight in a high-speed elevator when it starts to drop, or on a roller coaster during the big downward curve. Your body feels as if it is floating upward and you have to grab something to hold you down.

What happens when an astronaut in a weightless condition wants to drink from a glass? How could this be accomplished? What would happen if the astronaut pushed against one of the walls of the spacecraft? What other kinds of things happen during weightlessness in the spacecraft?

If air were not circulated by fans inside a spacecraft, an astronaut would die of suffocation in his own exhaled breath. Air currents on the earth come about as a result of heated air becoming lighter and moving upward. But if the air in a spacecraft is weightless, then the carbon dioxide an astronaut breathes out would stay around his face and choke him to death. What would happen if you lit a candle in a weightless state? You can see that weightlessness makes a pretty good fire extinguisher.

How to Gain Weight in Space

Here's What You Will Need: A bucket, strong string, water, a phonograph turntable, a cardboard strip 1 inch wide and long enough to go all the way around the turntable, tape, and a marble.

Here's What to Do: It is a good idea to do this experiment out-of-doors—just in case! Make sure that the string you use is strong enough to withstand a sharp pull. Tie the string securely around the handle of the bucket. Place some water in the bucket. Holding the string firmly, start to swing the bucket around in a circle. If you swing the bucket fast enough, the water will be forced against the bottom even when the bucket is upside down.

To see another example of this kind of outward force, attach the cardboard strip with tape around the edge of the phonograph turntable to form a rim. Start the turntable rotating, and place a marble near the center pole. Note which way and how fast the marble rolls. Try spinning the turntable at different speeds to see the effect.

Of course, you really did not make gravity in this demonstration. You substituted another force in its place. This outward pushing force is called centrifugal force. It is caused by the rotation or spin of an object. Can you tell what happens to the amount of this force when you make the turntable move faster?

Some scientists have designed a space station in the form of a kind of spinning doughnut. How would you construct rooms in this kind of station? Where would the floors and ceilings have to be located?

Are there any other ways man might move around a space

station without floating? What would be the advantages and disadvantages of using magnetic shoes to keep an astronaut on the floor?

At takeoff, an astronaut must withstand many g-forces. In orbit or outer space, he must get used to zero-gravity or weightlessness. Do you think you would make a good astronaut?

How Fast Is Your Spaceship?

Here's What You Will Need: A lead weight, string, a clipboard, paper, a ruler, a pencil, and a friend to help with this project. *Here's What to Do:* Insert a piece of paper onto the clipboard. Tie one end of the string to the lead weight. Place the other end of the string under the clip so that weight hangs just below the bottom of the board and is able to swing freely. Hold the board in an upright position, allowing the weight to stop swinging and come to a rest. Suddenly start walking rapidly, carrying the board. Observe what happens to the weight and the position of the string.

How would you know when a craft changes its speed in space? On the earth we can use an instrument that moves when in contact with the ground, water, or air, like a speedometer. But space has none of these elements that the craft moves past.

Newton's First Law of Motion states that an object remains at rest, or in the same kind of motion in a straight line, unless acted upon by some other force. The force that acts to keep an object at rest or in motion is called inertia. An increase in the speed of motion is called acceleration. The instrument used in space to measure a change in speed or direction is called an accelerometer. It uses the principle of inertia.

Here you can use your clipboard to demonstrate how an accelerometer functions. Wait until the weight stops swinging. Move slowly. Is the weight deflected to the same point as when you moved rapidly? Rule vertical lines on the paper 1 inch apart. Starting from the middle, number each line consecutively to the edges of the paper. You can see that the farther away from the center the weight moves, the greater the change in speed.

Can you think of how you can tell about changes in direction with an accelerometer?

Have a friend on a bicycle or on skates hold the accelerometer as he moves at a constant speed. How does the weight hang now? How does an accelerometer's reading differ from a speedometer's reading?

Saturn Calling

Here's What You Will Need: A toy train transformer (see below), bell wire, two wooden or plastic rulers, and earphones.

Here's What to Do: Wrap about 100 turns of the bell wire around each of the rulers. Leave about 24 inches of wire loose at each end. Connect the leads (wires) of one ruler to the terminals of the toy transformer. Supply the coil with 2–6 volts A.C. (Note: Make sure that you are *not* using a transformer-rectifier that supplies D.C. rather than A.C.) Connect the second set of leads from the other ruler to a set of earphones. Hold the coils a foot apart.

Turn the second coil until the hum in the earphones is at its weakest. Move the first coil in a different direction. Line up the second coil for the weakest hum again.

The first coil is acting as a radio-wave transmitter. The radio waves are broadcast at the frequency that electricity comes into your house power supply, usually sixty cycles per second. The second coil acts as the antenna for a radio-wave receiver. It picks up the sixty-cycle hum. The position where reception is faintest is called the null situation.

Special navigation transmitters are called radio beacons. How could you "home" in to a radio beacon? What would tell you when your craft leaves its course?

If you have a portable radio, you can experiment with the same principle of radio location. Tune in a distant AM station with a weak sound. Rotate your portable in a circle. The sound should be faintest at one point. This is the null position. Modern portable radios usually use a ferrite-stick antenna. In that case a null is obtained when the station is lined up with a stick. Special radios with rotating antennas are often sold to small boat owners for this kind of radio navigation aid.

Radio signals travel through space at the speed of light, 186,000 miles per second. Yet even at that great speed, radio signals from the Pioneer space probe took eighty-five minutes to reach Earth from Saturn. Tracking stations of NASA's Deep Space Network located in California, Spain, and Australia sent out 10,000 radio commands to Pioneer in the two-week period when Pioneer was close to Saturn. Pioneer will remain in touch with Earth at least through the mid 1980s.

Danger: Meteoroids Ahead

Here's What You Will Need: Pebbles and rocks of various sizes up to about $\frac{1}{2}$ inch in diameter, plaster of paris, a flat box or basin, a sheet of aluminum foil, a sheet of plastic food-wrap, and string.

Here's What to Do: Cover the bottom of the flat box with a layer of wet plaster of paris to a depth of at least 2 inches. Drop different-size rocks from a height of 1 foot onto the surface of the plaster. Increase the height to 2 feet, and drop other rocks. Also try throwing the rocks at various angles.

Use a sheet of aluminum foil as a shield to cover the plaster. Keep the foil away from the surface of the plaster by bending it over the sides of the box and tying it in place. Try dropping rocks onto the foil shield. Finally, use a sheet of plastic food-wrap as a shield instead of the foil.

Meteoroids are chunks of rock or metal speeding through space. The impact of the rocks on the plaster of paris is similar to the impact of meteoroids on the surface of the moon. Look at the kinds of craters made by dropping the rocks. Do they look like the craters you have seen in photographs of the moon's surface?

Is a crater the same size as the rock that made it? Does the size of the crater depend upon the speed of the rock when it hits the surface? How does the angle of impact change the way the crater looks?

Spacecraft in flight need some protection from meteoroid strikes. A thin layer of metal or other material held slightly away from the hull is one method of slowing down the meteoroids and lessening their effect. A good shield will absorb most of the meteoroid's energy of motion before it reaches the hull.

Empty Space

Here's What You Will Need: A 1-gallon can that has a tight-fitting screw cap, pot holders, water, an electric hot plate, a balloon, and a wide-mouthed Pyrex jar with a top (the jar must be made of Pyrex because it will be heated).

Here's What to Do: Make sure that the can is rinsed and clean. Place about one-half cup of water in the can. Heat it over the hot plate until the water is boiling rapidly for a few minutes. CAUTION: *Use the hot plate with care. Turn it off as soon as you have finished with it.* Using pot holders, remove the can from the heat and cap it promptly. Allow the can to cool. What happens to the can?

For the second part of this demonstration, blow up the balloon just enough to separate the sides, and close off the balloon with a knot. Place a small amount of water in the Pyrex jar and heat it over the hot plate. After the water is boiling rapidly, drop the balloon into the jar and cover the jar tightly. Remove the jar from the heat and let it cool off. What happens to the balloon inside the jar?

At sea level on the earth, air exerts a pressure of 14.7 pounds against every square inch of our bodies. This means that many tons of air are pressing against our entire bodies' surfaces all the time. But an equal pressure of air and fluids inside our bodies pushing outward prevents us from being crushed under this great weight.

The demonstrations in this project show what would happen if this balance of pressure is upset. The steam from the heated water drove most of the air from the can. When the can was capped, the water inside condensed, leaving a much lower pressure. How does this help to explain why the walls of the can caved in?

Much the same thing happened inside the Pyrex jar. What happened to the pressure inside the jar when the steam cooled? Why did the balloon in the jar expand at that point?

What would happen to people in space if they have no protection from the lack of air pressure around them? What are some ways that people can be protected in low-pressure surroundings? Can you tell how a space suit is similar to a deep-sea diving suit?

The Problem of Water

Here's What You Will Need: Ice cubes, water, food coloring, a wide-mouthed jar and cover, and a saucer.

Here's What to Do: Fill the jar with ice cubes. Add water to fill in the spaces, then add a few drops of coloring and cover the jar tightly. Place the jar on a saucer. Let the jar and saucer sit on a table for a few minutes. Observe what forms on the outside of the jar.

The air in your room has water vapor in it. But the water vapor is usually not present in amounts large enough to bother you. If there were no way to get rid of the water vapor in a spacecraft, it would rapidly become very uncomfortable and finally dangerous. You can see how this might feel by sitting in a closed bathroom while hot water runs continuously from the shower.

The water droplets on the outside of the cold jar came from the water vapor in the air, not from the inside of the jar. How does the coloring help you tell that the water vapor in the air was cooled when it came in contact with the jar? It condensed and turned into water, leaving the air less humid.

That would be desirable in a spacecraft, but a single jar of ice cubes cannot do much. Cold coils, such as in a refrigerator or in an air conditioner, can condense a lot more water vapor. Not only can electric cooling coils do a better job in freeing the air of water vapor, but they can be set to go on and off to maintain just enough vapor in the air to be comfortable.

An air conditioner in your home lets condensed water run off outside. But in a spacecraft, the water can be used again and again. Condensed water is pure water and perfectly good for drinking or for any other needs.

Of course, using condensed water again and again is nothing new. It happens all the time right here on the planet Earth. Do you know how all of us depend on water evaporating and condensing? Lakes, streams, rivers, oceans, clouds, and rain are all parts of a large spacecraft. We call that large spacecraft the planet Earth.

The Problem of Carbon Dioxide

Here's What You Will Need: Calcium hydroxide or calcium oxide (inexpensive chemicals found in many chemistry sets), water, a glass, a drinking straw, 3 or 4 jars with covers, plastic tubing, and a two-holed rubber stopper to fit the jar top (or you can use some plastic clay).

Here's What to Do: Add enough calcium hydroxide or calcium oxide to the water in a jar so that some is left on the bottom after the rest dissolves. Close the jar tightly and allow it to stand for a day.

When you return after a day, pour off the clear liquid at the top into another jar and keep this jar tightly closed. The clear solution you have is called limewater. You can discard the rest of the contents of the first jar.

Pour a little bit of the limewater into a glass. With a drinking straw, bubble your breath into the limewater. After a while, it should turn milky white. Put the glass containing the limewater aside for later observation.

Next set up the other two jars as in the diagram, placing some limewater in each jar. Place the rubber stopper in one jar, and bubble your breath through a tube into one of the holes. A tube from the second hole should lead into the second jar of limewater.

When we breathe, we exhale carbon dioxide. Carbon dioxide is not harmful in small amounts. On the earth, plants use carbon dioxide to make food and oxygen in a process called photosynthesis. In a spacecraft, carbon dioxide must be prevented from building up and becoming dangerous to the astronauts.

The carbon dioxide in your breath reacted with the limewater. This is what made the limewater turn milky white. After a while the white material settles to the bottom of the glass. The carbon dioxide you breathe out is now part of that white solid material. The white material is called calcium carbonate. The chemical reaction that took place is this: calcium hydroxide + carbon dioxide   calcium carbonate + water.

Compare the color of the limewater in the two jars. Which shows more of a reaction? How does this show that limewater can dispose of carbon dioxide? In the next experiment, you'll see another way to rid a spaceship of carbon dioxide.

Plants in Space

Here's What You Will Need: A clean wide-mouthed jar with a plastic cover, water plants such as elodea, two or three pond snails, water, and candle wax.

Here's What to Do: Make sure that the jar is clean. Rinse it free of all traces of soap. Fill the jar almost to the top with pond water or water from an aquarium. If neither of these sources are available, draw water from a tap and let it stand in an uncovered container for at least 48 hours.

Place several sprigs of elodea in the water along with the pond snails. Make sure that the water plant is green and firm. A rotting plant is soft to the touch and a darker green color. It will decay very quickly in the jar.

Use a tight-fitting cover to close the jar. Seal all around the edges with melted candle wax. Keep the jar in a well-lighted place near a window, but not in direct sunlight for any length of time.

One way to carry food and oxygen on a large spaceship would be to design a closed system containing plants as well as the astronauts. Briefly, the system would work around the idea of the plants supplying some of the food and oxygen, while the astronauts would supply the carbon dioxide and other materials needed by the plants.

In the closed-system aquarium that you have set up, the plants and the snails each provide something that the other needs. You may see bubbles of gas forming on the leaves of the plants during the day. The gas is oxygen. The snails use the oxygen and eat the plant material. In turn, the snails give off carbon dioxide and wastes that are used by the plants for growth and to make more oxygen.

One kind of plant that might be considered for long space trips is a microscopic green algae called chlorella. Under intense light, the plant multiplies very rapidly. When taken from the water and dried, chlorella can be made into a powder that can be used as a source of food. During growth, chlorella gives off a great deal of oxygen. Still another plant that is possible for long trips is the common corn plant.

Of course there are many problems to solve before a spacecraft could be made self-sustaining. Can people live on the plants grown on such a trip for a long period of time? Wouldn't such a diet become very monotonous even if it did contain enough nutrients? How many such plants and how much equipment would be necessary to set up such a closed life-support system?

The chances are that such a system will not be used until people stay in space for very long periods of time. But since scientists have solved the problems of going into space, they can probably overcome the difficulties in making a life-support system.

Magnetic Fields in Space

Here's What You Will Need: Two bar magnets, string, a compass, and an empty shoe box.

Here's What to Do: Tie the string to each end of a bar magnet. Attach the string to some object in the room so that the bar magnet is suspended in the air and can rotate freely. When it stops turning, note the direction in which it points. Tap it gently to start it turning. When it stops, again note the direction.

Bring the other bar magnet near the suspended one and see what happens. Finally, put a bar magnet in the shoe box. Move the compass around the outside of the box. What happens to the compass needle? Try to detect the magnetic field around the box.

Space probes and manned spacecraft carry instruments to detect magnetic fields around other planets. One such instrument is called a magnetometer. You showed the principle of a magnetometer when you worked with a freely swinging bar magnet. A compass works on the same principle.

The earth is surrounded by a magnetic field. Curved lines can be drawn to make a picture that shows the shape of the field. The lines are called magnetic lines of force. When a freely suspended bar magnet stops swinging, it always points along the lines of force. Use the compass to find out the direction in which it points.

Venus has been found to have a very weak magnetic field, possibly only one-thousandth as strong as the earth's field. Can you explain how a magnetometer in a space probe might have discovered this?

When space probes such as Mariner IV flew close to Mars, the magnetometer did not change position. Can you tell what that showed? The Voyager space probes showed Jupiter and Saturn have very strong magnetic fields. Many astronomers believe that there are magnetic fields in space between the stars. Can you tell how will we find out about these things?

What happens when you move the compass around the shoe box containing the bar magnet? Can you think of how you could use the changes in the compass's direction to draw a map of the magnetic field around the box? Try placing the box atop a sheet of paper and drawing lines in the same direction as the compass lines up. Does a magnetic field also extend above and below as well as on a flat surface? Where is the field strongest? Weakest? Try moving the compass all around and see.

Is Anything Listening?

Here's What You Will Need: A pencil and paper, and a friend to help you.

Here's What to Do: Suppose that there is a civilization on a distant planet that could pick up television signals from the earth. How could you devise a picture language that could be understood by an alien intelligence?

As a first step, try drawing a series of shapes that could be universally recognized as symbols for numbers. Then think of how you could explain how other shapes stand for addition, subtraction, and so on.

Try out what you devise by presenting the series to some friends. Tell them to pretend that it is a message from another civilization and that they have to decode it.

Any distant alien civilization that can pick up television signals from the earth should be able to figure out a consistent picture language. Philip Morrison, a Cornell University physicist, has devised such a system. Here, for example, is how he might send the problem $1 + 4 = 5$:

Can you decipher the symbols used? Try writing another problem in the same kind of picture language. Present this language to your friends and ask them to decode it.

Once the distant television viewer has discovered how to receive the pictures correctly, we could then send out regular pictures that could transmit any information we wanted. One difficulty is: How do we know if someone is listening? How could we recognize a signal that they send out as a reply?

Astronomers are aiming radio telescopes at all parts of the sky. So far they think that they have picked up radio waves from natural sources only. They hope to recognize a radio signal from an intelligent being by its regularity or by some other feature such as a pattern like the one of the space language shown above.

There is still another difficulty in communicating with a planet or a distant star. Radio waves travel at the speed of light, 186,000 miles per second. On earth that is very fast. But even at that speed, radio waves will take years to reach even the closest stars. Can you imagine saying hello—and then waiting one hundred years for an answer?

Star Light, Star Bright

Here's What You Will Need: A piece of iron or steel wire, a cork, a ruler, a gas burner on a stove, and a pot holder.

Here's What to Do: You can purchase iron wire in a hardware store. Picture-hanging wire can also be used. Cut off a 10-inch length of wire. Insert one end into the cork. Make a loop of the other end. Hold the cork end with a pot holder and place the loop into a gas flame. Keep the loop in the flame as it turns colors. CAUTION: *Do not touch the iron wire until it has cooled off.*

This demonstration is best carried on in a darkened room. The heated iron will start to glow. At first it glows red. Then as it gets hotter, the color changes. Which color does it glow at its hottest?

Generally, blue-white stars are the hottest, while red stars are the coolest. Our sun, a yellow star, is somewhere in between these extremes. The spectrum of a star is also related to the temperature of the star. The color and spectrum of a star help astronomers learn much about the star's age and composition.

Star Tracks

Here's What You Will Need: A candle or an alcohol lamp, matches, table salt, Epsom salts, baking powder, a cardboard shoe box, two index cards, tape, a scissors, and a diffraction grating. (You can buy an inexpensive diffraction grating set in cardboard from a scientific supply company such as Edmund Scientific Company, 300 Edscorp Building, Barrington, New Jersey 08007.)

Here's What to Do: Caution: Work this experiment in the kitchen sink because it involves lighted matches. At one end of the box cut a hole a bit smaller than the grating. Tape it over the hole. At the other end of the box, cut a hole $\frac{1}{4}$ inch wide and about 1 inch long. Tape the two index cards over the hole so that the edges form a very narrow slit.

Light the candle and point the slit end of the box at the flame. Look at the flame through the diffraction grating. You should see a color fringe on each side of the slit. If the colors appear only at the ends of the slit, untape the grating, turn it 90 °, and retape it to the box. Sprinkle each of the substances on the flame as you look through the grating.

Each element, when it is heated enough to become a gas, sends out only a certain set of colors. A scientist can recognize an element by the colors emitted when it is burned.

To identify the element, a thin beam of its emitted light is sent through a diffraction grating. The grating separates the colors in the light and forms a spectrum. This kind of spectrum is composed of a series of bright lines spread out according to the colors.

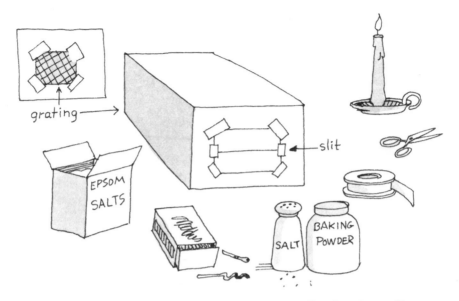

For example, sodium when heated gives off a bright yellow color, calcium gives off an orange-red, and lithium gives off a crimson color. Gas-filled lamps of each of these elements are used to produce different colored lights.

Are You Ready For Space?

Here's What You Will Need: You and your friends.

Here's What to Do: Make a list of the conditions that people must have if they are to live in space. How do they go about solving the problems of air, temperature, food, gravity, and excess radiation?

Now think about the other effects that space may have. What about the problems of noise and shaking during launch and reentry? What about the loneliness in a spacecraft or on the moon?

What happens when you are crowded into a small space with a group of other people? Do you ever become irritated and angry with them?

Could you sleep in definite time slots? Could you stand the sensation of no day or night?

Think of how you would go about experimenting with each of these aspects of space travel. Perhaps you can think of a way you could simulate aspects of space travel for you and your friends.

Try to devise a test that you can take, such as a large group of math questions in addition and multiplication. Take the test under normal conditions, and compare your results under the conditions of space travel that you set up. For example, how would you do on this kind of test in a very small crowded room with lots of noise? How would you do on this test after spinning yourself around for a while? Think of other ways you could test the effects of your space simulation.

Would you and your friends like to go on a space trip for days? For weeks? For years? What kind of people would volunteer for a space trip to a distant star?

Some of the more distant journeys may take generations. Whole families would go. Youngsters would be born in space and learn how to control the craft and what their mission is. In turn, they would teach their children and their children's children. What do you think of such a trip? Would you go on one if you knew that you could never return to Earth?

Glossary

Ablation: removal.

Ablation shield: a shield that melts away from a spacecraft because of the atmosphere's friction.

Acceleration: an increase in the speed of motion.

Accelerometer: the instrument used in space to measure a change in speed or direction.

Altitude: the height of an object from a surface.

Antenna: an object made of metal used to send and receive radio signals.

Axis: the line around which a spinning object spins.

Centrifugal force: an outward pushing force caused by the rotation or spin of an object.

Chlorella: a microscopic green algae (a source of food and oxygen).

Corning Ware: the commercial name of cookware made of Pyroceram.

Diffraction grating: a glass or polished metal surface with lines cut into the surface, used to produce a spectrum.

Elodea: water plants.

Filter: a strainer-like device for getting rid of solid impurities such as dust particles.

Frequency: the number of times radio or electrical waves repeat themselves during a specific period of time.

Friction: the rubbing together of two surfaces.

g-force: the increase of the force of gravity.

Hour: sixty minutes or 3,600 seconds.

Inertia: the force that acts to keep an object at rest or in motion.

Law of Motion, First: Newton's principle stating that an object remains at rest, or in the same kind of motion in a straight line, unless acted upon by some other force.

Law of Motion, Second: Newton's principle stating (1) the greater the force on an object the greater its change in speed or direction, and (2) the heavier an object is the less its change in speed or direction.

Law of Motion, Third: Newton's principle stating that for every action there is an equal and opposite reaction.

Life-support system, closed: a way of making a spacecraft self-sustaining by using plants to supply food and oxygen, while astronauts supply carbon dioxide and other materials needed by plants.

Liquid hydrogen: a rocket fuel made by cooling hydrogen to a very low temperature until it becomes liquid.

Liquid oxygen: a rocket fuel made by cooling oxygen to a very low temperature until it becomes liquid.

Magnetic field: the presence of a magnetic force detectable with a magnet.

Magnetic lines of force: curved lines drawn to show the shape of a magnetic field.

Magnetometer: an instrument used to detect magnetic fields around planets.

Meteoroids: chunks of iron or rock that travel through outer space.

Meteors: the glowing gases formed when a meteoroid enters the atmosphere and heats through friction (also known as shooting stars).

Mile: 5,280 feet.

Newton's Laws: see Law of Motion

Null situation: the position of an antenna at which reception is faintest.

Photosynthesis: the process by which plants convert carbon dioxide and sunlight into food and oxygen.

Pitch: the up-and-down motion of a spacecraft.

Pyrex: glass specially treated to withstand high temperatures.

Pyroceram: a material used to make cookware that can stand not only high temperatures, but can also be put into water while red hot and not crack.

Radio beacons: special navigation transmissions of radio signals.

Roll: the rotating motion of a spacecraft.

Rotation: the spin of an object around its axis.

Shield: a layer of material surrounding a spacecraft for protection against heat or meteoroids.

Shooting stars: see Meteors

Spectrum: the separation of a beam of light into its component colors.

Speedometer: an instrument that measures speed by moving when in contact with the ground, the water or the air.

Thrust: the forward-directed force of a rocket as a reaction to the rearward ejection of fuel gases at high speeds.

Weightlessness: the condition of objects in a spacecraft when a gravitational force is counterbalanced by the ship's motion.

Yaw: the side-to-side motion of a spacecraft.

Index

ablation shield, 28
acceleration, 39
accelerometers, 39–40
air
    circulation of, in spacecraft,
        34
    water vapor in, 50
air conditioners, 50
airplanes, friction and, 25
air pressure, 47–48
alcohol, water in, 16
alien civilizations, 62–63
altitude, formula for, 13
antennas, 42–43
Apollo missions, 28
astronauts
    apparent weights of, 31
    dangers to, 31, 34, 48, 53
    g-forces and, 31
    life-support systems for, 56–
        57
    protection of, 31, 48, 53
    weightlessness and, 34
axis, 22

blue-white stars, 65

calcium, 68

calcium carbonate, 54
calcium hydroxide, 53, 54
calcium oxide, 53
carbon dioxide, 53–54
    chemical production of, 10
    danger of, 34, 53
    plants and, 53, 56
centrifugal force, 36
chemical reactions, 7, 10, 54
chlorella, 57
closed life-support systems, 56–
    57
cold coils, 50
colors
    of elements, 67–68
    in spectrums, 67–68
    of stars, 65
communication
    with alien civilizations, 62–63
    by radio, 42–43, 62–63
    with spacecraft, 43
compasses, 59–60
condensed water, 50–51
corn, 57
Corning Ware, 29
craters, 45

Deep Space Network, 43

diffraction grating, 67

Earth
    air pressure on, 47
    gravitational pull of, 19–20
    magnetic field of, 59
    moon of, 2, 20, 45
    orbit of, 22
    as spacecraft, 51
electricity, 42
elements, 67–68
elodea, 56

ferrite-stick antennas, 42–43
filters, 16–17
First Law of Motion, 39
free fall, speed of, 4–5
frequency, of electrical and radio
        waves, 42
friction, 25–26, 28
fuels
    chemical, 8
    impurities in, 16
    solid vs. liquid, 8

Gemini missions, 28
g-forces, 31, 37
gravitational pull, 19–20, 31, 33
    centrifugal force vs., 36

Halley's comet, 2
heat
    friction as cause of, 25–26
    of stars, 65
heat shields, 28–29
hour, number of seconds in, 5
hydrogen, liquid, 8

impurities, in fuel, 16
inertia, 39

Jupiter
    gravitational pull of, 20
    magnetic field of, 60
    ring around, 2
    Voyager space probe of, 2, 60

launches, 19
    g-forces in, 31
    of match rockets, 4–5
    of water-powered rockets,
        13–14
Laws of Motion
    First, 39
    Second, 5
    Third, 7, 10
life-support systems, 56–57
light, speed of, 43, 63
limewater, 53–54

liquid fuels, 8
lithium, 68
living conditions, in space, 70–71

magnetic fields, 59–60
magnetometers, 59
Mariner IV space probe, 59
Mars
   magnetic field of, 59
   Mariner IV and, 59
   surface of, 2
   Viking spaceships and, 2
Mercury missions, 28
meteoroids, 25, 45
meteors, 25
mile, number of feet in, 5
moon (Earth's)
   gravitational pull of, 20
   surface of, 2, 45
Morrison, Philip, 62
motion, *see* Laws of Motion

NASA, Deep Space Network of, 43
Newton, Isaac, laws of, 5, 7, 10, 39
null situation, 42

oxygen
   liquid, 8
   plants and, 53, 56–57

photosynthesis, 53
picture language, 62
Pioneer space probe
   pictures transmitted by, 2
   radio signals from, 43
pitch, 22
plants
   carbon dioxide needed by, 53, 56
   oxygen produced by, 53, 56–57
   in spacecraft, 56–57
pressure, air, 47–48
Pyrex, 29
Pyroceram, 29

radio
   signals, 43, 62–63
   waves, 42, 62
radio beacons, 42
red stars, 65
rockets
   fuel for, 8, 16
   made with matches, 7–8

(cont.)

    thrust of, 10–11, 16
    two-stage, 13–14
    water-powered, 12–14
roll, 22
rotation, 36

Saturn
    magnetic field of, 60
    moons of, 2
    Pioneer probe of, 2, 43
    radio signals from, 43
    Voyager probe of, 60
Second Law of Motion, 5
shields
    against heat, 28–29
    against meteoroids, 45
shooting stars (meteoroids), 25
signals
    radio, 43, 62–63
    television, 62
sodium, 68
solid fuels, 8
sound, speed of, 25
Space Age, 2
spacecraft
    air circulation in, 34
    carbon dioxide on, 34, 53, 56
    Earth as, 51

(cont.)

    friction and, 25, 28–29
    heat shields of, 28–29
    life-support systems for, 56–57
    magnetic fields detected by, 59
    meteoroid shields for, 45
    plants in, 56–57
    shields for, 28–29, 45
    stabilization of, 22–23
    water on, 50
    weightlessness on, 33–34, 37
space probes
    magnetic fields detected by, 59–60
    Mariner IV, 59
    Pioneer, 2, 43

    Voyager, 2, 60
space shuttle
    heat shield materials of, 28
    speed of, 25–26
space stations
    centrifugal force of, 36
    as launch points, 19
space suits, 48
space travel, 70–71
spectrum

(cont.)

    colors in, 67–68
    of elements, 67
    of stars, 65
speed
    of falling objects, 4–5
    of light, 43, 63
    measurement of, 4–5, 39–40
    of radio signals, 43, 63
    of sound, 25
speedometers, accelerometers
        vs., 39–40
spinning objects, 22–23, 36
stars
    colors and spectrums of, 65
    temperatures of, 65
static-test stands, 10
sun
    color and spectrum of, 65
    gravitational pull of, 20

television signals, 62
temperature
    friction and, 25–26
    of stars, 65
Third Law of Motion, 7, 10
thrust
    impure fuel and, 16
    measurement of, 10

(cont.)

    of rockets, 10–11, 16
transmitter, radio-wave, 42
two-stage rockets, 13–14

Venus, magnetic field of, 59
Viking spaceships, 2
Voyager space probe, 2, 60

water
    in alcohol, 16
    condensed, 50–51
water-powered rockets, 12–14
water vapor, in air, 50
weight, g-forces and, 31
weightlessness, 33–34, 37

yaw, 22
yellow stars, 66

Books for Reading and Research

Baker, David. *Space Shuttle.* Crown, 1979

Cipriano, Anthony J. *America's Journeys into Space.* Messner, 1979

Knight, David C. *The Moons of Our Solar System.* Morrow, 1980

NASA. *Pioneer Saturn Encounter.* NASA, 1979

   . *Images of Mars,* 1980

   . *Voyager Encounters Jupiter.* NASA, 1979

Ross, Frank, Jr. *The Space Shuttle.* Lothrop, 1979

Shurkin, Joel N. *Jupiter—The Star That Failed.* Westminster, 1979

Simon, Seymour. *Look to the Night Sky.* Viking, 1977

Simon, Seymour. *The Long View into Space.* Crown, 1979

Taylor, G. Jeffrey. *A Close Look at the Moon.* Dodd, 1980